SCARY STATES (OF MIND)

HORROR IN CONNECTICUT

by Alex Giannini

Consultant: Debbie Felton
Professor of Classics
University of Massachusetts
Amherst, Massachusetts

BEARPORT PUBLISHING

Minneapolis, Minnesota

Credits

Cover, © Kim Jones, © Karen Grigoryan/Shutterstock, © KathySG/Shutterstock, and © Weerachai Khamfu/Shutterstock; 3, © Kim Jones; 4-5, © Felix Lipov/Shutterstock, © Laura Stone/Shutterstock, and © Dan Hanscom/Shutterstock; 6-7, © Frank. C Grace and © Lario Tus; 9, © Gracie Ann Matisyn; 11, © Tony Spera - nespr2@yahoo.com; 13, © AmityPhotos / Alamy; 14T, © autsawin uttisin; 14B, © pra_zit; 15, © Brian Wegman; 16, © Peter Dedeurwaerder; 17T, © jannoon028; 17B, © Sandor Szmutko; 19, © Allan Wood Photography; 20, Courtesy Library of Congress; 21, Courtesy Library of Congress; 23, © Shanshan0312; and 24, © Valentina Proskurina.

President: Jen Jenson
Director of Product Development: Spencer Brinker
Editor: Allison Juda
Designer: Micah Edel
Cover: Kim Jones

Library of Congress Cataloging-in-Publication Data

Names: Giannini, Alex, author.
Title: Horror in Connecticut / by Alex Giannini.
Description: Minneapolis, Minnesota : Bearport Publishing Company, [2021] | Series: Scary states (of mind) | Includes bibliographical references and index.
Identifiers: LCCN 2020000565 (print) | LCCN 2020000566 (ebook) | ISBN 9781647470722 (library binding) | ISBN 9781647470821 (ebook)
Subjects: LCSH: Haunted places—Connecticut—Juvenile literature. | Ghosts—Connecticut—Juvenile literature. | Connecticut—Miscellanea—Juvenile literature.
Classification: LCC BF1472.U6 G525324 2021 (print) | LCC BF1472.U6 (ebook) | DDC 133.109746—dc23
LC record available at https://lccn.loc.gov/2020000565
LC ebook record available at https://lccn.loc.gov/2020000566

For more information, write to Bearport Publishing, 5357 Penn Avenue South, Minneapolis, MN 55419. Printed in the United States of America.

CONTENTS

Horror in Connecticut

Connecticut is home to rolling hills, horse farms, cute villages, and miles of sandy beaches. But there are horrors that **lurk** at night. Spooky spots include one of the world's most haunted graveyards. Not far from there awaits a terrifying museum of the **occult**!

Get ready to read four terrifying tales about Connecticut. Turn the page . . . if you dare.

THE WHITE LADY

Union Cemetery, Easton

Union Cemetery is said to be America's most haunted graveyard. A rusted gate leads into the 400-year-old cemetery. Old, broken headstones are scattered about the grounds.

Union Cemetery

But visitors to Union Cemetery, beware. The graveyard is home to the dreaded White Lady, a restless spirit known to haunt the grounds—and beyond!

The White Lady has long, black hair and wears a flowing, white dress. Drivers have caught ghastly glimpses of her walking on the road toward the cemetery.

Sometimes, the White Lady even jumps in front of passing cars. Drivers slam on their brakes, fearing they've just hit a person. But when the terrified drivers get out of their cars, no one is there!

A pair of glowing eyes is said to watch from behind the gravestones of Union Cemetery. This spirit is known as Red Eyes.

A Deadly Doll

The Warren's Occult Museum, Monroe

Ed and Lorraine Warren were two of the most famous **paranormal investigators** in the world. During their time ghost hunting, they collected many haunted **artifacts**.

They put these frightening objects in their basement and turned it into a museum. On display were a vampire's coffin, demon masks, and other weird items.

The Warren's Occult Museum

The Warrens investigated more than 10,000 spooky cases during their careers as ghost hunters.

A rag doll named Annabelle was the Warrens' most famous item. The doll once belonged to a woman named Donna, who claims she saw it move on its own. Donna said the doll even tried to strangle one of her friends!

Terrified, Donna called the Warrens. They locked Annabelle in a case in their museum. One day, a visitor made fun of the rag doll. On his way home, he died in a motorcycle crash. Did Annabelle put a **curse** on him?

The Warrens claimed the doll was possessed by the spirit of a dead girl named Annabelle Higgins.

Ghosts in the Funeral Parlor

Snedeker House, Southington

In 1986, Allen and Carmen Snedeker made a shocking discovery in the house they had just bought. In the basement, they found many strange things. There were sharp tools and a rusted **gurney**. They even found a pit that was used for **draining** blood! The Snedekers realized their new house had once been a funeral parlor.

Snedeker house

Allen and Carmen tried not to worry. They turned the basement into a bedroom for two of their sons. But at night the boys saw ghostly visions.

Plates and silverware from the dinner table mysteriously vanished or moved. One day, Carmen took out a mop and bucket to clean the kitchen floor. When she looked down, the bucket was filled with a bloodred liquid!

Ghost hunters Ed and Lorraine Warren said the house was possessed. The family eventually moved out.

Ghostly Lighthouse Keeper

Penfield Reef Lighthouse, Bridgeport

On December 22, 1916, lighthouse keeper Frederick Jordan got ready to go home for the Christmas holiday. He left his assistant behind at Penfield Reef Lighthouse and boarded a small boat.

On its way to shore, Frederick's boat **capsized**, and he drowned in the dark water. To this day, other keepers claim Frederick's spirit still roams the lighthouse.

Frederick's drowned body was not found for several months. It washed ashore nearly 20 miles (32.2 km) away from the lighthouse.

Penfield Reef Lighthouse

After Frederick died, Frederick's assistant Rudolph Iten took over as keeper. Two weeks later, Rudolph woke up with the feeling of someone standing over him. He saw a misty figure walk out of the old bedroom.

Since then, other people have also seen ghostly figures. Some have heard the sound of phantom footsteps. Many have seen lights switch on and off at all hours. Is Frederick's ghost still performing his duties as keeper?

An illustration of the lighthouse from 1874

Stairs in the Penfield Reef Lighthouse

Spooky Spots in Connecticut

GLOSSARY

artifacts (ART-uh-fakts) objects of historical interest that were made by people

capsized (KAP-sized) turned over in the water

curse (KURSS) something that causes evil or injury

draining (DRAYN-ing) removing liquid from something

gurney (GUR-nee) a stretcher to carry a hospital patient or dead body

lurk (LURK) secretly hide or lie in wait

occult (AH-kult) of or related to the supernatural

paranormal investigators (pa-ruh-NOR-muhl in-VEST-uh-gay-torz) people who study events or collect information about things that cannot be scientifically explained

INDEX

READ MORE

Markovics, Joyce. *Chilling Cemeteries (Tiptoe Into Scary Places).* New York: Bearport (2017).

Phillips, Dee. *Nightmare in the Hidden Morgue (Cold Whispers II).* New York: Bearport (2017).

LEARN MORE ONLINE

1. Go to **www.factsurfer.com**
2. Enter "**Horror in Connecticut**" into the search box.
3. Click on the cover of this book to see a list of websites.

ABOUT THE AUTHOR

Alex Giannini is a writer who also works in a public library. In his free time, he likes to hunt for thrilling ghost stories.